A BRIEF DISCOURSE
ON THE
DEFINITION
AND
TENETS
OF
FINANCIAL JUSTICE

A BRIEF DISCOURSE
ON THE
DEFINITION
AND
TENETS
OF
FINANCIAL JUSTICE

JOE HOLBERG

This book is designed to provide accurate and authoritative information on the subject of personal finances. While all of the stories and anecdotes described in the book are based in reality, most of the names are pseudonyms and some situations have been changed slightly for educational purposes and to protect the individual's privacy. This book is sold with the understanding that neither the Author nor the Publisher is engaged in rendering legal, accounting, or other professional services by publishing this book. As each individual situation is highly unique and individualized, questions relevant to personal finances and specific to the individual should be addressed to an appropriate professional to ensure that the situation has been evaluated carefully and appropriately. If you require legal advice or other expert assistance, you should seek the services of a competent professional. Furthermore, it is sold with the understanding that neither the Author nor the Publisher is offering advice tailored to any specific portfolio nor rendering investment advice. The publication references performance data collected over many time periods. Past results do not guarantee future performance. Additionally, performance data, in addition to laws and regulations, change over time, which could change the status of the information in this book. This book solely provides historical data to discuss and illustrate the underlying principles. No warranty is made with respect to the accuracy or completeness of the information contained herein, and both the Author and Publisher specifically disclaim any liability, loss, or risk which is incurred as a consequence, directly or indirectly, of the use and application of any of the contents of this book.

Published by Blog Into Book
1871: Holberg Financial
222 W Merchandise Mart Plaza
Chicago, IL 60654

Copyright © 2018 by Holberg Financial

All rights reserved. Neither this book, nor any parts within it may be sold or reproduced in any form without permission.

Printed in the United States of America

To Jessica

Proceed whilst daring greatly.

CONTENTS

Introduction 9
Definition 13
Tenets of Financial Justice 17
    I   Access to Information and Support 19
    II   Wage Equality 23
    III Expense Equality 27
    IV The Reasonable Expectation of
          Wealth Accumulation 33
    V   Access to Cost-Transparent and Non-Predatory
          Financial Products and Services 37
    VI A Framework and Legal Limitations on the Use of
          Credit Scores and Reports 43
    VII Tax Equality 49
Moving Forward 53
About the Author 55

Introduction

ACCORDING TO THE Merriam-Webster dictionary, justice is defined as "the quality of being just, impartial, or fair."[1]

There have been many efforts throughout time to establish justice in a variety of domains and many of them, if not all, are arguably ongoing as a pure attainment of impartiality or fairness are impossible to attain in the perfect sense as humans are inherently partial and unfair, even if slightly so in the best of circumstance. Our own actions in constructing systems that we build may seek to be just, but our implementation, execution, and maintenance thereof are done so via human limitations and guided by those who, even at best, are still imperfectly able to bring about a pure, unadulterated sense of justice even when explicitly attempting to do so. Can an individual or group of individuals improve upon and bring about a greater sense of justice? Absolutely so: we are capable of continuous improvement and time allows Martin Luther King Jr.'s "Arc of the Moral Universe" to ever be bent towards justice and yet, we cannot reach perfection. To believe otherwise is to be blinded by an idealized utopian vision of both society and human morality.

---

[1] https://www.merriam-webster.com/dictionary/justice

The causes that have driven us as a collective society towards greater levels of justice are not only inspiring, but they are instructive. Justice has been sought at every turn across the globe and it is something that is easily felt deep within the marrow of the mind - people tend towards justice, freedom, and equality, even if their current situation and circumstance confines them to the opposite pole of repression, inequality, or unfairness.

In the United States specifically, we have a long history of seeking justice, starting with the beliefs set forth in the Declaration of Independence. Namely, the rebellion against the Crown and system that sought to maintain a hierarchically superior position over those people who wished to be treated equally in the citizen sense as well as on the economic and political levels. As the early colonists were not treated equally, they rebelled, fought, died, and eventually won independence. And while the claim that "all men are created equally" was enshrined in our Founding Documents, it wouldn't be until slavery was abolished at the hand of Lincoln, women's suffrage was won in the early 20th Century, and not until the Civil Rights movement spurred along national sentiment and legislation granting African Americans and other minorities the unalienable rights and abilities that they too hold as inhabitants of this Country, that we would have actually made meaningful progress towards legitimizing the claim that put into practice the words that were penned nearly a quarter of a millennia before.

This progress was long coming, it took effort and it took an incomprehensible amount of suffering, pain, and loss and yet, it was worth it. The benefits of increased justice to society and to individuals is immeasurably positive. The ripples of fairness are not those caused by a pebble tossed into a lake, rather, they are the societal tidal waves that lift all boats higher. It is a force that reverberates in perpetuity and it creates an energy whose effect is so ubiquitously great that it cannot be measured. In effect, justice is worth seeking to an ever greater degree as we advance as a society.

Ideally, after all we have learned to date, we would welcome change and embrace efforts to bring about more justice in society, yet we know, by all historical accounts, that subsequent attempts to bring fairness and impartiality and introduce it more largely to an ever increasing number of people will be met with, at best, neutral skepticism, and, almost certainly, with open resistance and hostility. The status quo is a powerful anti-pole to increased justice and those who currently benefit from the current societal architecture will be at the forefront leading the counter-resistance to those who want to see greater levels of fairness, impartiality, and justice.

In laying down the definition of Financial Justice and the tenets thereof, I do so knowing that many will not only reject it, but will go to lengths within their means to discredit it, undermine it, and stop its progress. Only a deep sense of naivete would allow me to believe otherwise. It is with the hope and the confidence in people and society that this discourse will proceed knowing that it will be a long road ahead, but it is one that will ultimately move us towards a more fair, impartial, and just society at large and specifically, as it relates to personal financial matters.

Definition

FINANCIAL JUSTICE (N): the equal and fair ability for all individuals in society to pursue a financially independent, secure, and healthy life.

In analyzing each part of the definition, we first turn to the clause "equal and fair ability" insofar as the level of equality needs to be extended ubiquitously across multiple dimensions, including, but not limited to geography, socioeconomic status, gender, race, age, creed, and any other variable that is known to be protected under common law and to those that are reasonable extensions that are not yet codified. The fairness mentioned simply means that we cannot adhere to systems or practices that unfairly exploit, take advantage of, or knowingly or unknowingly capitalize on different individuals or groups of people. Currently, there is a deep-seated level of unfairness and inequality built into our financial constructs where legitimate, barely legitimate, and illegitimate actors alike utilize unfairness and an unequal application of their practices to continue to gain.

Turning to the next clause, "for all individuals in society to pursue," I will clarify that this is not an economic argument for any system such as collectivism, shared wealth nor is it for the promotion of anything akin to socialism or communism

- these ideas have vast flaws and are contrary to the capitalism that drives America forward. It is not an argument for redistribution of wealth, nor is it for a Robinhood approach to taxation, necessarily (although a greater degree of taxation on the wealthiest in society would certainly tend, at this point, to represent more equality and fairness in our system). The centrality lies in the verb "to pursue" in that each person should have the reasonable expectation that they can pursue with as much fervor, hope, and ambition as anyone else - just as we notably pursue happiness, as enshrined in the Declaration of Independence. Primarily, individuals should not be hampered nor promoted because of certain traits or circumstances that are beyond their control. Only those that are in direct proportion to aspects they in fact do control should determine the outcome. Essentially, in pursuing, one should be able to attain, if in fact we have created a more meritocratic system.

Finally, in looking at "financially independent, secure, and healthy life," it is to say that each of these should be the outcomes for one who pursues fervently and arduously. It does not promise riches, it does not guarantee wealth, nor does it insure against the pitfalls of life, but rather it promises that the pathway is both equal and fair to all those that pursue these outcomes. In being independent, I mean to imply that one has a great degree of choice in their financial circumstances insofar as the choices made are those made independently of financial pressures or limitations. This warrants an example. An independent individual will be able to choose whether or not they want a mortgage. Now, they may not be able to purchase a home with cash, per se, but having the choice to continue to rent versus obtain a mortgage represents a level of financial independence and therefore choice, that is allowing them to pursue life. Of note, independence should not be conflated with the idea of being debt-free. A great amount of independence and choice can and will be had while simultaneously holding debt and to think otherwise is ignorant. However, extending the example, if said individual faces an extortionary rent environment while being offered a disadvantageous, costly mortgage, then this person is not only subjected to unfairness and inequality, but has had their financial independence impugned. What about all of those renters who wish to own a home? Are they not less independent because they cannot buy a home? Not necessarily, if they cannot afford it now, then they can save for the future. If they are unable to save because they haven't learned how to save well, the onus for improvement is on them and they still have a level of financial independence in the absence of home ownership, for example. However, if they are systematically unable to save because they have not the income or the mandatory expenses are too high, then they have not an appropriate level of financial independence as they do not have the choice to save. Admittedly, this is tenuous ground as parsing out mandatory expenses and determining how much savings is possible given income, does not have a clear cut answer and is subject to debate and to individual circumstances.

 In turning to security, every individual should have a level of surety in their lives that allows them to handle to vicissitudes and mercurial nature in life. Security allows an individual to weather a financial rainstorm. Security manifests itself in a variety of ways, but can generally be encapsulated by one's ability to rise and meet the unexpected financial events in life. Most commonly, this is referred to as an Emergency Fund or Rainy

Day Fund and it has time-tested merit as being able to cover unexpected events is one of the hallmarks of financial security that millions of Americans have not yet achieved. Abstaining from a detailed analysis of what in fact financial security entails, it will suffice to say that financial security is that which allows one to be prepared for and handle both the expected and unexpected events (financial and otherwise) that crop up across time.

Finally, in looking at health, we are tasked with creating a fair and equal ability for individuals to become financially robust and healthy. We cannot accept a level of financial anemia or frailness among those in society just as a doctor would not accept a course of non-treatment to those patients who had curable ailments. The health sought is one of improvement and betterment insofar as the individual is able to meet his or her financial goals over time should they prove reasonable and realistic. To deny people their goals because of an unfair and unequal system is appalling and should be rectified as quickly as possible. Health is also a multifaceted, holistic assessment insofar as it is not measured solely based on income, savings, or housing, per se, but it seeks to assess financial health along as many dimensions as is relevant to an individual and may include the above as well as many others. These dimensions, while many will be standard across time, are not fixed and there should be a fluidity of inclusion to make sure that health is measured as accurately as possible.

Tenets of Financial Justice

THE CORE TENETS of financial justice are access to information and support, wage equality, expense equality, the reasonable expectation of being able to save and build long term wealth, access to cost-transparent and non-predatory financial products and services, a framework and legal limitations on the use of credit scores and reports, and finally, tax equality that is progressive, balanced, and non-onerous. In turn, let's examine each in further detail to fully flesh out the pillars that constitute an overall understanding of how to create a more financially just system.

I

Access to Information and Support

FOR SEVERAL HUNDRED years, the full body of personal financial information has been known, studied, and applied and yet, it is nearly perfectly sequestered in the hands and minds of those with the greatest amounts of means and wealth in society. Largely, this is a result of being able to afford financial guidance and wealth management services that are profitable both to the recipient (the client, by growing wealth) and the advisor (the companies providing such products and services, who charge for their efforts). In our capitalistic society, there is both a supply and a demand for financial information and at the highest socioeconomic levels and yet, the profitability shrinks to zero when attempting to inform and support those with less. Thus, there is a demand, but a very limited supply outside of the highest socioeconomic brackets where even relatively high earners still struggle to obtain solid information and support, let alone the ability for moderate and below earners to achieve the same.

Wealth management has an inherently positively reinforcing cycle to those who can afford it insofar as if you can afford advice, you can become better off in perpetuity being able to afford more and more specialized levels of information, expertise, and skills. However, if you can't afford advice, then you are largely unable to find high-quality, relevant information on how to obtain a better sense of financial security and success. There is nothing inherently wrong with obtaining advice and information on how to build and preserve wealth, in fact, it is encouraged and the accumulation of wealth is a economic imperative for both individuals and society at large - even if unequally distributed - for having wealth in society increases the overall quality of life for everyone, even if not everyone feels the rising quality of life equally. However, when members or groups of people are unable to access and utilize information for their own understanding and advancement, then there is a disbursal issue that needs to be rectified as information is freely shared with non-reductionist properties and when more people hold higher levels of information from the knowledge corpus, both individuals and society improve at a greater rate, allowing more people to be caught up in the positively reinforcing cycle more readily.

In the 21st Century, with the explosion of technology and raw information, this lack of ability to access and comprehend information may seem quaint or outdated at best, irrelevant or wrong at worst, however, the outcomes we see in society are in large part, a direct consequence of lack of information and support, even if the internet has made information ubiquitous. There are several underlying issues that continue to restrain access and usage of financial information that in turn can be applied to one's situation and circumstance.

First, ubiquity does not imply clarity. Just because it exists, does not mean it is organized or digestible. This is nearly a self-evident point for anyone who has searched for information and been flooded with millions of search results. Secondly, for those who do access information, there is a varying degree of quality and some information obtained either digitally or via more traditional channels (books, directly from people, etc) can be dubitable at best, completely wrong at worst and being subject to varying (and potentially indiscernible) degrees of quality information is rife with issues commonly explained as a "market for lemons" as the classical economic example goes. Thirdly, and most importantly, even if one has access to high-quality information, it does not imply that one has the ability to synthesize and act upon this information. A simple analogy proves this point: having a nuclear physics textbook does not mean one will become proficient in the application and construction of nuclear power plants just as having an anatomy book does not equip one for brain surgery. Avoiding the fallacy of equating access to mastery is key to understanding that access to information and the specialized support through industry expertise are two distinctly separate aspects, both of which are necessary in order to apply them to one's circumstance. Medically speaking, knowing you have an ailment does not imply that you understand the diagnosis, let alone the course of treatment much in the same way knowing you have financial needs does not imply you know what actions to take nor what end result to pursue.

The first tenet is crucial as information in the absence of support leaves individuals ill-equipped to act; support in the absence of information leaves individuals following blindly a hand that may or may not be capable or aligned to serving the interest of the recipient; and an absence of both leaves exposed the individual to the mercurial hands of Fate, which is the least preferred of the states enumerated here.

Furthermore, the first tenet is arguably *primus entre pares* (first among equals) as the proportional level of importance given all of the tenets of financial justice are most bolstered and furthered when individuals and society are able to expand and attain both information and support - this, as a driving force, propels all the others most strongly and if we were to concentrate efforts on any, increasing access to information and support would be the favored tenet.

II

Wage Equality

IN PURSUING THE worthy objective of wage equality, it must first be recognized that the objective is to not only eliminate a gap in earnings between the sexes, but the underlying objective is to eliminate the "power gap" between the sexes. This unequally distributed power is a force that currently suppresses the popular desire to establish wage equality, however, if harnessed and channeled, the power dynamics of our society could be used to more rapidly work towards wage equality. This power inequality negatively manifests with institutions having skewed leadership metrics at the executive level across government, academia, business, and civil society. In a society of equal proportionality between men and women, every single type of institution, when weighed in aggregate, has more male leadership representation than women. Given the nature of power, society will have to channel and champion the popular notion at all levels that leadership equality is essential to driving wage equality and while the later can be improved in the absence of the former, it will not only be more difficult, but likely impossible to attain fully. This leads to the conclusion that addressing wage equality without training an eye on power equality will be less successful and perhaps futile. It will take a conscious effort by those oppressed women to be the strongest advocates for the cause and they must necessarily rally the privileged men who hoard power disproportionately to be allies and advocates. The power-holding males who understand that a short term acquiescence of power and wages ultimately is not a zero-sum game and that more diverse leadership and workforces coupled with a rising progress towards wage parity actually enhances both men and women, will be the ones who not only most strongly champion the notion of wage equality, but will be beneficiaries just as the women they support will be. It is unfortunate that the onus of bringing about wage equality rests on the shoulders of women, but even a cursory glance at history will demonstrate that in order for an oppressed group to gain equality it is necessary is to be their own biggest champion. Men have taken and selfishly (knowingly or unknowingly) kept their unfair share of power and wages for the whole of human history and no one can live in the blissful ignorance that the status quo position will be voluntarily yielded, no matter how prized the ideal outcome of such an action would be, it must be taken directly by those that wish to better their circumstances.

While equal jobs require equal pay, by law, a large part of the systemic wage inequality is driven by societal expectations, stereotypes, and reinforced messaging of "gender roles" and while this portion of the calculus is omitted (and rightfully so, to obtain the most valid conclusions) in empirical research surrounding wage equality, it is an exacerbating variable that furthers financial injustice mainly for women, but for men as well. For women, they are cast as secretaries, fashion and style designers, waitresses, and any number of other positions that are overly sexualized and stereotyped as jobs "for women." This ancient societal casting reaches back to the primitive "hunter-gatherer" model of society with men roaming the earth in search of animals to slay with women calmly stooping over land with vegetables and fruits growing serenely - open any elementary textbook for confirmation of this. Men are not the only software engineers and computer scientists. Men are not the only construction workers or Fortune 500 executives. While the media diet continues to be one of the worst promulgators of these stereotypes and gender roles, nearly everyone else is largely complicit in the endeavor to train boys, girls, men, and women that there is a cleavage between the two genders insofar as we dress baby boys in blue, baby girls in pink, and that's just how we start to corrupt the next generation at infancy. The body of research is too extensive to enumerate and, like unequal leadership and power dynamics across institutions, the societal expectations play directly in to reinforcing the gender dichotomies in the workplace which then manifest ultimately as the "wage gap."

III

Expense Equality

WHILE "WAGE EQUALITY" is quite a familiar notion and one that has in recent years been more widely covered and discussed, there is no discussion whatsoever on the flip side of wage equality. Namely, "expense equality" as it is conceived of here, is the first instance that I am aware of, that will shed light on a persistently unequal, yet uncovered corner of financial injustice. Expense equality mirrors its counterpart, wage equality, in that it is measured primarily in gender terms (although no doubt the analysis would hold for race and ethnicity). Expense equality refers to the extent to which regular and necessary expenses are distributed in an uneven manner among a population. In analyzing a typical expense profile, one can quickly eliminate expenses that are shared between genders: housing, utilities, internet, food, transportation, education, and entertainment such as movies, streaming services, etc. These expenses are generally consistent across the population and men and women don't face discrepancies in these areas unless mainly by choice (although, I'd be the first to say that future research will likely dispel the expense equality between housing and transportation costs. Namely, that women in fact do pay what could be called a "safety premium" for housing and transportation to avoid more risky and less safe modes of transportation or living locations as women are also much more likely to be victims of crimes such as theft, muggings, harassment, battery, assault, and more. This risk can be mitigated by avoiding less safe neighborhoods or public transit, both of which generally cost less, but increase risk factors, hence the "safety premium" paid to avoid it). Once the generally similar expenses are removed and cancelled out, one can look at the expenses that are generally different between men and women. It is important to note here that these differences of expenses are limited to *necessary* expenses and do not include indulgences or excessive spending (men spend more on cars and video games, for example, but as these differences are easily demarcated as non-necessary (luxuries), they are excluded from the expense gap). This is a tricky grey area, no doubt, as will quickly be demonstrated. In looking at typical expense profiles, one would include several unequal categories such as health and beauty, clothing, and hygiene. The important dimension to note, in the following breakdown, is that of these unequal expense categories, that there is both a necessary expense component for each and a non-necessary expense component. The argument is not that the entirety of the expense or category, for that matter, is one or the other, but that a proportion of the expense is. An example will best highlight this: on average, women are held to a significantly different standard for health and beauty than men are. The level to which women must strive to be seen as healthy and beautiful by society and individuals, as was discussed in the wage equality section, is built and reinforced not only by our collective history, but by our (almost always) unrealistic expectations of what women look like in the workplace, when socializing, and virtually everywhere at all times - it is shaped by media, news, magazines, men, women, family, friends, enemies, and the pressures to conform extend beyond the merely psychological or social. The health and beauty standard that women are held to can impact their employability, job performance reviews, promotion ability (and rate of promotion), likeability, perception among peers and colleagues, compensation and this only scratches the subtle and not-so-subtle forces that lead women to spend billions of dollars annually on health and beauty products, regimens, and services ranging from hair styling, facial makeups, lip glosses and lipsticks, lotions, creams, eye and eyelash products, nail care (fingers and toes), skin care, and more. It's not that women *want* to incur more expenses than men in the health and beauty realm, but it is that society and individuals *expect* and *demand* that they do, otherwise the penalties for not participating and looking the part can add up emotionally, psychologically, socially, *and* financially.

Now, this is not a carte blanche excuse for *all* health and beauty expenses women incur to count towards the expense gap, but it is the realization of the real cost of the societal expectations we place on one gender and not the other. Therefore, we can conclude that *some* expenses related to health and beauty for women are beyond their direct choice should they wish to not be ostracized and penalized by society. To what degree or proportion this is a forced expense versus an elective one will be determined by future research, but for now, we can confidently conclude that women face an unjust increase in expenses in the health and beauty category while admittedly, this is to look at a narrow category.

The same logic can be applied to clothing. There is obviously some basic level of clothing necessary for men and women just as there is an excess, however, like health and beauty, women are held to a higher standard when it comes to variety and type of clothing that vastly exceeds men's clothing standards (men can essentially wear a very limited rotation of shirts and pants with small, if any, negative consequences in the workplace and world). Women on the other hand must have slacks, dresses, skirts, blouses, shirts, camisoles, shawls, jeans, *and* they must have accessories from totes and bags, to purses and clutches, not to mention earrings, bracelets, necklaces, and a healthy rotation to make sure they aren't seen as "plain, typical, predictable, unfashionable, or boring." Of these perceptions that can damage a woman's professional and personal life, which carry the same type of financial consequences already enumerated, they are precisely the descriptions that men not only do not have to adhere to, but often benefit, with slight variation, from when described as "steady, calm, crisp, tidily dressed, dependable, sturdy." These subtle nuances amount to and cause the perpetuation of the expense gap that women face from a clothing dimension.

Finally, at the raw biological level, hygiene costs are fully absorbed by women whereas men have virtually zero corollary expenses, unlike health and beauty and clothing. Men do not menstruate, women do. Not only does society demonize the natural, biological rhythms of women (most ironically as it is the precise mechanism necessary for giving life), but it places the full onus of feminine hygiene on women. There is no equivalent hygiene cost for men. Women have to buy pads, tampons[2], and other items that help them navigate the world and the cost each month can add up significantly with a small box of tampons or pads being $5, $10, or more just for the basic necessities. Of all of the categorical discrepancies feminine hygiene is least grey and paints a stark "black and white difference" that gives the most definitive example of the expense gap and the corresponding inequality. Furthermore, given the clarity with which one can see the expense inequality that women face related to feminine hygiene, it could reasonably be argued that this issue could be addressed at the policy level whereby women are compensated at some level to help reduce the unequal expenses they face. While many will oppose this based on ideological differences, if we think about the collective negative effects of both wage and expense inequality, this line of policy making would not only seem reasonable and affordable, but would only measure a small (but worthy) victory in the name of financial justice at large, when everything else is considered.

Expense inequality is happening not only in the gender dimension, but the racial and ethnic ones as well. These will most likely roughly follow the same type of discrepancies that research has shown to be evident in terms of wage inequalities. Namely, that minorities face further increases in expenses on average than even women face. If this proves not to be true, all the better as it would mark a rare score for minorities in not

---

[2] Assuming it costs $10/month for tampons or pads, an 8% annual growth rate, and a 25 year initial phase from age 13-40, the value missed is $10,869. Taking that principal then growing at the same rate from 41-67 (another 26 year time period, assuming no other periods (pun intended)), the total lifetime cost of tampons is $80,391.

being even more further disadvantaged in society than they already are given the constructs in which we operate as a nation.

IV

The Reasonable Expectation of Wealth Accumulation

BUILDING WEALTH IS difficult, even for the relatively well off. Markets change, wages and employment situations change, and life calls for many seen and unforeseen expenses that ebb and flow as rapidly as the tides themselves. Given the caprices and variations that are inextricable from life, building and accumulating wealth is inherently challenging even for the savvy, the saver, and the strategist.

In identifying wealth accumulation as a tenet of financial justice, it is important to note that the degree to which one may achieve wealth is relative in that there is not some ubiquitous and absolute threshold that exists. It will vary based on factors both internal and external to the individual. Furthermore, a financially just world will embody the reasonable expectation that one can acquire wealth. This does not create the mandate that in order to be just, everyone must have some measure of wealth as we must account for those who do have the ability to accrue wealth, but given their values and decisions, use it towards their own ends and designs.

There are two keys to use as frameworks for facilitating wealth accumulation. First, what are the mechanisms that are hindering wealth accumulation? This list will stretch long as it contains the time-tested behavioral choices that individuals make that slow wealth accumulation such as spending too much and saving too little. It will also include systemic factors such as not understanding how to build wealth, being exposed to opaque and predatory financial products and services (expounded later), or being subject to the previously unjust tenets such as wage inequality, expense inequality, and other large scale forces.

The second mechanisms are the ones that facilitate wealth accumulation. Again, individual behaviors and choices that can harm can also help. Creating patterns, systems, and behaviors that systematically - over the long run - compound is the surest way to controlling and advancing wealth creation. The system has tools, vehicles, and resources embedded in it that will further propel wealth accumulation. From tax-advantaged accounts and market accessibility to compounding investments and strategic financial guidance, the route to wealth accumulation can be lubricated by currently available products and services as well as our continued societal disposition built upon free market and capitalist principles.

As it stands now, there is a massive wealth disparity between races and ethnicities with whites having a higher net worth *14 times greater than* blacks, *10 times greater than* hispanics, and *1.18 times more* than Asians.[3]

---

[3] According to the US Census Bureau, Wealth, Asset Ownership, & Debt of Households Detailed Tables: 2013 (https://www.census.gov/data/tables/2013/demo/wealth/wealth-asset-ownership.html)

Compounding this, the wealth disparity among men and women is not only present, but a logical outcome from the wage and expense gaps. Single men have over *3 times as much* wealth as single women.[4]

This disparity - as well as the nature - of wealth accumulation itself (or debt accumulation, for that matter) is closely tied to the compounding of interest in that it is the fastest way to build wealth over the long run. Interest works both in favor when growing assets and against when taking on more debt and we can relate compounding interest to physical acceleration. While building wealth is slow going at first, like a ball rolling down a slope, it builds both speed and acceleration. For wealth, it takes years, decades, and even generations to exponentially capture the accelerating nature of this asset growth and on the flip side, debt accumulation can occur even more rapidly as the interest rates associated with debt, on average, are higher than on the asset building side of the equation. Mathematically speaking, when one begins to build wealth, the virtuous upwards cycle can quickly take over which makes not only the accumulation, but the perpetuation of wealth more probable. Sadly, the vicious cycle of debt accumulation works with equal force and can build quickly, spirally out of control as assets are eroded, debt accumulated, and ultimately, bankruptcy incurred. Obviously the nuances and reality of life do not lend themselves perfectly to extreme wealth nor extreme poverty, but they do yield insight into the cyclical perpetuation of both prosperity and poverty across generations which can be freeing if wealth is obtained and stifling in the absence thereof.

---

[4] According to the Asset Funders Network publication by Mariko Chang: *Women and Wealth*. (http://www.mariko-chang.com/AFN_Women_and_Wealth_Brief_2015.pdf)

As we seek to create a more just environment for asset building, we have to focus on removing or mitigating the factors that hinder wealth accumulation while simultaneously enhancing and increasing access to the means of wealth building. Both of these dimensions need to combine together so that wealth can be most efficiently accumulated. It is worth noting that, generally, asset and wealth accumulation by any one person does in fact raise the overall wealth and prosperity across society, however, that does not imply that it is *proportionally* felt across everyone. For example, while society may be better off in aggregate by the increase in overall wealth by an already wealthy individual, that does not mean that individuals with less or no wealth proportionally benefit in a manner that actually significantly improves their wealth accumulation prospects. In essence, we shouldn't slow wealth from accumulating, but we should avoid the unnecessary and inefficient concentration of wealth in too few pockets of society as this further exacerbates the disparities that are already entrenched.[5]

---

[5] For a more detailed description of the perils of concentrated wealth, see materials that discuss the Gini Coefficient (https://en.wikipedia.org/wiki/Gini_coefficient)

V

Access to Cost-Transparent and Non-Predatory Financial Products and Services

THE RAVAGES OF opaque financial products and services strip out tens of billions of dollars from people's pockets every single year. At bare minimum, finances can be challenging to understand from a conceptual or content standpoint. It takes effort to learn about and understand personal finances. But adding in the pernicious and confusing costs, fees, terms, and long-winded legal documentation can make finances feel like a tempest-tossed storm that threatens to sink the entire ship. There are too many financial traps that are laying out there waiting to exploit individuals than there is space to delineate them. However, a few brief points will help guide us to creating a more financially just environment where companies and individuals are prohibited from knowingly designing financial products and services that are not transparent nor predatory in nature.

In this age, we have to first understand the motive behind, and the incentive for, each product and service that we interact with. Companies and individuals that have or offer financial products and services are motivated to make money. That is the motive that drives both the financial sector as well as the economy at large, to think otherwise is to engage in willful ignorance. The incentives for products and services vary, but they generally fall into a handful of categories: charging a premium for a product, a fee for an account or service, by charging interest, or by servicing ads digitally or selling data. Every financial product or service must make money and the means to do so change in flavor and magnitude, but each carries this objective. In attempting to induce more cost-transparency, an individual, first and foremost, must be the first line of defense. The simple argumentation is that if one does not understand the financial product or service or its cost, then that individual is not adequately prepared to transact and adopt said product or service. No one would hop in the cockpit of a rocket ship without first becoming an astronaut, just as no one should elect for life insurances, investment products, bank accounts, loans, credit cards, etc without first fully understanding their design, their costs, and how they operate. Unfortunately, this is not a default position for many and the negative ramifications of engaging in financial products and services that have hidden or confused their fees and costs amounts to a parasitic extraction of money from individuals at best and a full fledged usury at worst.

The examples on the lower side of the socioeconomic spectrum are well known and documented: check cashing, payday loans and advances, refund anticipation loans (RALs) during tax season, wire transfers and remittances fees, usurious auto loans, expensive adjustable rate mortgages. Gary Rivlin has detailed these extensively in his excellent inspection of the predation that happens to low-income Americans in *Broke USA* and it is well worth the read. More systemically, much like the "food deserts" across America, both in rural and urban areas, there are, what I call, "financial deserts" whereby access to high-quality, low-cost, and transparent financial products and services is scarce to those without and concentrated near those that have. The pattern almost certainly has a high correlation with the known food deserts and while I do not know of a national effort to map the existence of financial deserts, we can take an educated guess that where you find Whole Foods, you will find Bank of Americas and high quality financial institutions around in abundance and where you find corner stores loaded with sugary foods and drinks, you will find the lecherous, low-quality, high cost financial outposts designed to strip out wealth from the already encumbered low-income Americans. Further census level research should be conducted as it was to establish and put a quantitative analysis around the notion of food deserts and we can only hope that this happens sooner rather than later to fully map out the costs and ramifications faced by those in financial deserts across the U.S.

The metaphorical buck doesn't stop there. Middle and upper income individuals face costly products and services as well. They are sold insurances they are not ready for or do not need at all (I term this being "over-insured"), they have retirement and investment accounts that are overpriced compared to lower-cost alternatives (this can add up to $30,000 or more in lost value over a lifetime[6]), they get access to credit then fall into debt paying, on average, over $1,000 in interest each year[7] and the list continues as individuals face financial products and services that are ripe for layering in costs at each step of the way. The hidden and high fees are just as prevalent in products and services that are designed for the higher socioeconomic marketplace as they are at the lower end of the spectrum and the sum total of these can easily surpass $100,000 of lost wealth over the course of an individual's lifetime. Yes, there is a cost of transacting, no one would deny this, but the costs themselves are far larger than they would be in a more cost-transparent and competitive environment where consumers understood fully the price they were paying to engage in such products and services.

While market forces will slowly encourage and reward business who tend towards cost-transparency, there is a glacial historical dimension that acts as a counterweight to the innovation and market principals that will benefit consumers. Namely, there are trillions of dollars of funds locked into existing products and services that have low cost-transparency and high fees. Trillions of dollars have been placed with these companies, who throughout the past were actually the competitive options given the marketplace at that juncture. However, these companies are currently relying on the stickiness of their legacy and the difficulties associated with the movement of money away from their expensive costs and to lower, better options that now exist in the midst of the greatest era of technological innovation the

---

[6] https://www.nytimes.com/2016/10/23/your-money/403-b-retirement-plans-fees-teachers.html

[7] https://www.nerdwallet.com/blog/average-credit-card-debt-household/

world has ever seen. This technological innovation is a boon to consumers writ large and especially so for those that actually migrate away from the historical high-cost financial companies to the new opportunities emblematic of the digital age in the financial space. Perhaps the largest and most notable example is active versus passive investing and wealth management.

Active management being once a specialized, niche, and valuable service was able to create trillions of dollars of wealth in the economy, for the better. At the most basic level, investors needed access to markets and specialized traders, brokers, and advisors who were able to facilitate and provide guidance that benefitted their clients. It worked for both consumers and companies. However, as theory, research, and the application of new ideas repeatedly and scientifically demonstrated that active wealth management was a strictly inferior allocation of money compared to the newly evolved and more widely available notion of passive management, the former became too costly and less efficient than the latter. Passive investing in the form of index and exchange traded funds have swept up trillions of dollars of assets as consumers and institutional investors (such as state funds, pensions, etc) have moved away from high-cost active management and their associated products and services. Active management still has a small roll to play in the economy as it is, arguably, a viable and valuable approach to those with complex investing needs, however, even Warren Buffett believes that passive wealth management is the best option for nearly everyone in the U.S.[8]

---

[8] https://www.bloomberg.com/news/articles/2016-05-02/put-buffett-s-advice-into-action-with-these-two-etfs

In closing, there are two factors to consider, which taken in tandem will accelerate our ability to weed out predatory and opaque financial instruments. First, individuals as financial agents, for themselves, need to start inspecting and inquiring about the products and services they interact with. This is easier said than done and, as a prerequisite, requires the first tenet of access to information and support to be in place to greater degrees over time. The market responds to consumer demands and the more demand there is for low-cost, transparent instruments, the more businesses will offer in this vein. This is just as slow of a mechanism for change as the second factor, which is direct policy and legislative changes that will work towards the ends of making sure that, if nothing else, consumers understand not only how, but how much, they are getting charged for the financial instruments they use. Right now, while struggling for its own existence, the Consumer Financial Protection Bureau (CFPB), is our country's greatest hope for the promotion of these goals. It has not only increased the level of transparency in many financial areas since its creation in the wake of the Great Recession, but it has established a comprehensive strategy of both educating consumers as well as promoting policies and legislation towards their protection. Towards these ends, change is coming, but the more active positions individuals take, the more rapidly it will come.

VI

A Framework and Legal Limitations on the Use of Credit Scores and Reports

CREDIT SCORES AND reports were initially designed to assess the ability of an individual to make good on the credit they utilized and therefore the debts that they had incurred. It's a relatively straightforward concept that simply attempts to figure out the likelihood of whether or not someone will uphold their end of the legal contract of borrowing funds. If someone paid back their debts and managed their debt and credit well, they had a good credit report and thus a good score. If not, then their score and report reflected this. The application was intended for the credit marketplace and it functioned reasonably well for decades.

This is hardly the case anymore. Credit scores and reports are now being used and applied to completely inappropriate areas that it was not intended to be applied. Most notably, when you submit a rental application it is becoming more and more widely practiced to check your credit report and score as well. Rent is not a form of credit. It is a pre-paid monthly expense. The argument posed by property management is simple, your credit score is a predictive guide as to whether or not you will pay your rent. However, not only is it outside the bounds of the applicability of determining whether or not you are likely to pay back a *debt*, which rent is not, but it takes on a more insidious and veiled dimension as it unfairly acts as a proxy for racial and ethnic discrimination. FICO, the main generator of credit scores will argue that their scores are not unfairly discriminating against minorities,[9] however, what they fail to recognize, and how credit scores are systematically used to discriminate against minorities, is that, in combination with other factors such as the well-documented "redlining" that banks use to target low-income and minority communities for subprime (aka expensive and disadvantageous) mortgages and other financial products, there is a pernicious self-reinforcing echo chamber whereby minorities face discriminatory products which damage their scores, then the scores are used to further exclude and discriminate against them. Which one comes first is irrelevant as they are forced into a credit and debt trap that *because of their credit scores* are virtually impossible to escape. Unlike a dwindling savings account which one can replenish with time and persistence, rebuilding your credit score is not only extremely difficult to do, but it is *by design* nearly impossible to know how to actually build your score outside of general guidelines. Imagine trying to pursue a healthy diet and exercise regimen by receiving the advice "eat healthy, exercise,

---

[9] http://www.fico.com/en/blogs/risk-compliance/do-credit-scores-have-a-disparate-impact-on-racial-minorities/

and try hard." This is effectively the extent to which one can know how to rebuild damaged credit. Furthermore, there is a multi-billion dollar industry dedicated to "credit repair" that is loosely regulated and predatory in the extreme. Not only do the companies offering these services charge ridiculous fees, they almost never actually get the results that they claim they will and they leave already struggling individuals high and dry with no recourse after stringing them along with false promises.

Not only can credit be used to exclude Americans from housing and as a proxy for race with lethal precision akin to Jim Crow laws, but it is being further abused as an indicator of job-worthiness and employability. This is outrageous and disgraceful. No one should ever be denied employment based on credit. Period. This is a non-negotiable position and the irony is that those seeking employment with low credit scores and challenging financial situations are the ones who stand to gain the most from employment opportunities. The cruel, unfair, and highly unjust application of the use of credit scores as a measure of employability is as corrupt and morally wrong as it is prejudiced and discriminatory.

There is a second factor that needs to be considered related to credit scores which as it stands, is subject to generally unrestricted market forces. Namely, loans, credit, and financial debt products for those with low credit scores are obviously more expensive. This is not inherently a problem. Supply, demand, and repayment rates drive the mathematical calculus of prevailing interest rates offered to individuals across different credit tranches. While you can and should expect to pay more for access to credit when you have a lower score, it is riddled with the aforementioned problem of being a proxy for race, but it is further exacerbated by companies that offer a wide array of subprime products who know that their consumer base has extenuating needs with a limited choice set. This combination makes consumers beholden to them and their usurious rates and extremely high cost financial products. The simple solution is to create legal caps on interest rates and fees. For example, only 15 states have enacted rate cap laws to stop the "payday debt trap" whereas only 6 have taken some steps to protect consumers against usury and exploitation. Embarrassingly, this leaves 29 states, *the majority in the U.S.*, with the unbridled ability to exploit consumers. In Minnesota you can face 200% interest rates, in California - where over 10% of the entire population resides - you can face 460% rates and in Texas, which makes Minnesota look benevolent, you can face 662% interest rates.[10] Car loans, payday loans, tax preparation providers, check cashers, and more are literally cashing in on the poor and those who have low credit scores (again, See *Broke USA* by Gary Rivlin for more details). It is not difficult to create legislation to protect vulnerable consumers who are locked in a downward cycle of borrowing to cover expenses then in subsequent rounds of borrowing, face higher costs in order to stave off the repayment of borrowing from previous rounds. This cycle can persist for years with no relief or viable alternatives even though hundreds if not thousands of concepts, legislation, and solutions have been proposed for decades.

In summation, the solutions are not only just and equitable, but will improve the prospects of millions for generations to come: stop allowing the usage of credit scores and reports

---

[10] http://www.responsiblelending.org/research-publication/map-us-payday-interest-rates

for both housing and employment, and safeguard against the future misapplication by narrowly defining what they can be used for. Further, create rate caps and regulation around usurious, exploitative, and prejudiced products and practices. Simple. Actionable. And proven to protect and improve the lives of millions of Americans. The debate is non-existent, the implementation shouldn't be.

VII

Tax Equality

THIS SECTION WILL not dive in to the litany of the tax code as it stands now, but rather will identify core pillars that can be used to inspect a given tax system to see if it is financially just and equitable. The three pillars of creating tax equality are to ensure that it is progressive, balanced, and non-onerous.

While we have a current tax system that is technically progressive, there are enough byzantine avenues to ensure that if you have means and wealth, that you can effectively pay little or no tax either as an individual or as a business entity. We need to weed out this ability by simplifying and streamlining the tax code. If you make more, you should pay more. This is the definition of a progressive tax system and it should be strived for. Hundreds of millionaires and billionaires have directly and outspokenly asked to be taxed more as low taxes and reductions in their tax burden will increase inequality.[11] They are not only admirable for their position, but this highlights that even the wealthiest realize that fueling inequality from less progressive tax systems is not in the best interest of increasing the financial

---

[11] http://fortune.com/2017/11/13/geore-soros-ben-jerrys-millionaire-billionaire-raise-taxes-congress/

health and prosperity in the US economy in the long run. Sure, they would benefit in the short run, none of them would deny this, but they are looking at the system at large and in the long run, hence their position. Not only would it ultimately benefit the economy at large in the long run, but it would immediately help middle and lower income Americans. This mass lessening on the average income earner as the wealthy continue to pay a progressive level of tax, would fuel growth in the economy as consumer spending will directly increase with a lower overall tax on middle and lower income individuals and families. This has been repeatedly been demonstrated as sound economic and fiscal policy.

The second pillar revolves around a balanced tax system. Being progressive is the first pillar, but we cannot sway too far in either direction against a balanced tax system. This has a see-saw effect to it whereby we should be looking at the proportional allocation of the tax burden across the income spectrum. The framework is simple enough: tax wealthy earners more, but not excessively, tax lower income earners the least, and tax middle income earners some. Using this framework, we avoid both shouldering the middle class with the vast majority of the proportional burden, but we do not crush the wealthy with European level taxation. The American system should still align itself with the capitalistic incentive to earn more as it creates wealth and raises overall GDP. In being balanced, taxes should be affordable at all levels which implies that many low and moderate income individuals and families may not pay any taxes at all and may in fact continue to receive the same (or more) credits and deductions such as the Earned Income Tax Credit (EITC), Child Tax Credit (CTC), Child and Dependent

Care Credit (CDCC), Savers Credit, and more. Middle income households will continue to pay a reasonably proportional amount which will compose a significant proportion of the tax base, and the wealthiest will contribute the highest share. The end goal is to make sure that the government revenues are sufficient (this abstains from a larger discussion of whether or not government expenses are currently appropriate) to fund federal, state, and local services which has been at the heart of the social contract in the U.S. since 1776. This analysis is devoid of numerics as the framework is a guide only. Needs change in society, socioeconomic composition changes, demographics shift, and the pillars themselves act as a lamp that we can hold up to shed light on the future as we feel our way forward.

The final pillar of tax equality is to ensure that the tax system is most generally non-onerous. This implies that as many individuals across society should not be unfairly burdened with a disproportionate tax requirement. The measure here, unlike the first two, is more absolute than relative. In asking whether or not the taxes faced are non-onerous, we have to look at the taxes that are paid and whether or not the taxes themselves detract from the individual or family ability to maintain a financially secure and successful household. From this standpoint, no wealthy individuals technically face an onerous burden as their quality of life and ability to retain their financial security and success is not jeopardized under the current system. Middle income Americans, who have faced an increasing cost of college for children, roughly static wages since the 1970's, and rising consumer prices are squeezed due to the external pressures and as such, the argument would go that there is some relief and alleviation that could come from a tax perspective for those middle class individuals and families nearer to the 25th percentile compared to the 75th percentile although the proportion and ultimate solution would be vastly more nuanced and complex than simply raising or lowering the taxable burden. Think tanks, policy experts, government agencies, as well as elected officials should work towards greater equality for both individuals as well as for the country at large. This means that whatever results will almost certainly have to be bipartisan, coalition driven, and fully vetted by the public (efforts which are, sadly, far fewer in number today than in previous generations).

Tax equality and the pursuit thereof is not going to be easy, but it is actually one of the tenets of financial justice that we actually have the most control over as our legislation and tax law is a direct output of the will of the people and therefore it is changeable given concerted and multidimensional efforts. Unlike wage equality and access to support, which are systemically impossible to change with legislation only, tax equality can be modified by people, all people, through both the pressures placed on elected officials as well as by the officials themselves.

Moving Forward

FINANCIAL JUSTICE CONTRIBUTES to the stability, the overall health, and the longevity of a given society and it should be looked at as one of many measures that are used to assess the moral, the civil, and the ethical character of a nation. When a society is financially unjust or is tending towards less financial equality, the risk of internal discord, strife, and, at worse, dissolution and civil war increase. Not only are there internal risks, but externally a nation is less innovative, competitive, and renowned. The international and geopolitical landscape will most favor those nations who directly create the most financially just and inclusive system for their citizens, which will have the positive externality of making the nation more respected and competitive globally. Time has well-documented the ill-effects of concentrations of wealth, financially corrupt and unfair regimes and systems, and the economic imperative and data alone are sufficient grounds for enhancing and promoting a greater sense of financial justice. This is not a matter that can be addressed by individuals alone. Business, institutions, and government must act as well. The responsibility of the individual to access information, seek wage and expense equality, and to build wealth is a key part of the equation to increasing the level of financial justice, but it cannot seen as a solution in isolation as we will have to approach this issue from all angles and from all levels of society.

Moving forward and deeper into the 21st Century and beyond, financial justice must be a definition and concept that is utilized to further the prospects of the United States. If we err in thinking that a laissez-faire approach to building an equal and fair ability for all individuals in society to pursue a financially independent, secure, and healthy life is the route to national prosperity, then we will see the foundations of our society and economy erode to the point where the notion of all that is America will be relegated to the history books which has been the case for all formerly great civilizations on earth.

We have the ability to further enhance an already dynamic, powerful, and beneficial system that works even better for hundreds of millions of Americans. With a greater sense of equality and fairness, we will surely find no limit to our successes individually and collectively, and that after all, is the American Dream.

About the Author

JOE IS ON a crazy mission to help hundreds of millions of Americans learn about their finances and build their financial health so they can reach their financial goals and dreams. He is the Founder & CEO of Holberg Financial, which helps thousands of companies, organizations, and employees across the country with an innovative technology platform and model that strives to be the polar opposite of the entrenched status quo. He is the author of "Rogue Finances: The "Un-system" Designed to Help You Become Financially Healthy, Successful, and Awesome"

His perspective is drawn from a variety of experiences including working at Google, teaching middle school math on the West Side of Chicago, and having created a loan underwriting system for the he Capital Good Fund, one of the country's largest microfinance organizations.

He lives in Chicago, where you can find him drinking coffee and reading books.

Also written by Joe Holberg -
Order on Amazon.com today!

JOE HOLBERG

ROGUE FINANCES

Grab a copy of Joe's last book, *Rogue Finances*, on Amazon.com today!

www.ingramcontent.com/pod-product-compliance
Lightning Source LLC
Chambersburg PA
CBHW030509220526
45464CB00006B/2724